LILLENAS®
DRAMA

I0893115

THANKSGIVING

PROGRAM BUILDER NO. 4

Creative Resources for Program Directors

Compiled
by KIM MESSER

lillenas
PUBLISHING COMPANY

PO Box 419527
Kansas City, MO 64141

Questions? Please write or call:
Lillenas Publishing Company
Drama Resources
P. O. Box 419527
Kansas City, MO 64141
Phone: 816-931-1900 • Fax: 816-412-8390
E-mail: drama@lillenas.com
Web Site: www.lillenasdrama.com

Executive Editor: Kim Messer
Supervising Editor: Kimberly Meiste
Manuscript Formatting: Karen Phillips
Cover Design by Brandon Hill

Contents

Recitations for Preschool 5

Recitations for Ages 5 to 7 6

Recitations for Ages 8 to 10 8

Youth & Adult Readings and Reflections 9

Scripture Readings 13

Programs & Services

A Service of Praise and Thanksgiving 17

Give Thanks to the Lord 19

Just What *Is* Praise? 22

Recitations for Preschool

On Thanksgiving

CHILD 1: It's fun to celebrate
Thanksgiving Day!
CHILD 2: The turkey with dressing is yummy.
CHILD 3: Plus all the other foods we enjoy
CHILD 4: That give us a happy tummy!
CHILD 5: But first, before we eat this feast,
CHILD 6: We bow our heads and pray,
CHILD 7: "Thank You, God, for Your faithfulness
ALL: Today and *every day*!"

by Dorothy Heibel

Our Wish for You

(A group of four-year-olds say together)

We're just four
But we're big enough to say
We wish you
a Happy Thanksgiving Day.

by Margaret Primrose

Turkey Cheer

(For a boy or girl.)

"Gobble, gobble," turkey cheer!
Thanksgiving Day is finally here!

by Evelyn Mika

Thanks to God

We thank You, Lord,
For Mother Earth
And the dear country
Which gave us birth.

by Dorothy Heibel

Thanksgiving Is Coming

(Use the Sunday before Thanksgiving. Follow this with a song of thanks that everyone can sing together.)

Thanksgiving is coming—
coming soon.
Please help us sing a happy tune.

by Margaret Primrose

Happy Hearts

With hope in our hearts
We pray and sing,
"Thank You, God,
For a *Happy Thanksgiving*!"

by Dorothy Heibel

Something to Say

We have something we all want
to say.
We wish you a Happy Thanksgiving
Day.

by Margaret Primrose

Recitations for Ages 5 to 7

Thank You, Heavenly Father

For all the ways You have blessed us,
With gifts from Your loving hand,
We give Thee thanks, dear Father,
From *all* in this beautiful land!

by Dorothy Heibel

Count Your Blessings

(The first verse should be spoken by one child. Each subsequent blessing may be spoken by ten different children. May close with song: Count Your Blessings.*)*

Thanksgiving Day is on the way;
It's time for celebration!
Count your blessings, one by one;
It's such a revelation!

One is family, two is friends,
Three is for God's care.
Four is home, five is health,
Six, God's always there.

Seven is heaven, eight is life,
Nine is God above,
Ten is when I start again
Counting God's great love.

by Evelyn Mika

A Prayer of Gratitude

Father, for all You have given us,
All bounty large and small,
We offer a prayer of thankfulness,
"Please bless us *one and all*!"

by Dorothy Heibel

Welcome!

Welcome! Welcome! Welcome!
Is all we have to say.
We want to let you know
We're glad you're here today.
Happy Thanksgiving!

by Margaret Primrose

A Blessing

CHILD 1: Help us understand, Lord,
The poor with whom we must share.
CHILD 2: Help us know how we can help them,
And show them that we care.
CHILD 3: For we are all alike to God,
Equal under the sun,
CHILD 4: And if we follow His guidance,
He'll bless us, *every one*.

by Dorothy Heibel

A Time to Thank God

This isn't just a holiday,
Not just a time to sing.
It's a time to thank the Lord
For the joy Thanksgiving
brings.

by Margaret Primrose

Grateful Hearts

With grateful hearts
We thank You, Lord,
For Your gifts
Of peace and love.
Please continue to bless
Our daily lives
With protection
From above.

by Dorothy Heibel

The First Thanksgiving

(Have children draw large pictures to go with this recitation.)

CHILD 1: How did the first
Thanksgiving begin?
CHILD 2: The Indians and Pilgrims
Were the reason.
CHILD 3: They met to share
The fruits of the earth,
CHILD 4: Thanking God for a
Bountiful season.

by Dorothy Heibel

Recitations for Ages 8 to 10

The Pilgrims

On Thanksgiving
We honor the Pilgrims:
That brave little band
Who sought freedom of worship
In an unsettled land.
Through many dangers
They sailed over the sea
To find religious freedom
For you
And for me.

by Dorothy Heibel

Thanksgiving Verses

(Each CHILD *recites a Thanksgiving Bible verse and all sing a song of thanks together.)*

CHILD 1: "This is the day the LORD has made; let us rejoice and be glad in it." (Psalm 118:24)

CHILD 2: "Give thanks to the LORD, for he is good; his love endures forever." (Psalm 118:1)

CHILD 3: "Thanks be to God for his indescribable gift." (2 Corinthians 9:15)

CHILD 4: "Give thanks to the LORD, call on his name . . ." (1 Chronicles 16:8)

CHILD 5: "Enter his gates with thanksgiving and his courts with praise . . ." (Psalm 100:4)

CHILD 6: " . . . give thanks to him and praise his name." (Psalm 100:4)

CHILD 7: "Give thanks in all circumstances, for this is God's will for you in Christ Jesus." (1 Thessalonians 5:18)

CHILD 8: "Sing to the LORD with thanksgiving . . ." (Psalm 147:7)

Now our class will sing a song of thanksgiving and praise: *(Insert song title)*

Suggested Songs: *This Is the Day*, by Less Garrett, Maranatha Music; or *Thank You Lord*, 3 verses, by Seth & Bessie Sykes, New Spring.

by Iris Gray Dowling

Reach Out to Your Brother

(For a boy or girl)

Thanksgiving is a time to care
And share with every one
The blessings you've been given,
The comfort, joy, and fun.

So, reach out to your brother
In a very special way.
Give food and care or fellowship.
Pass blessing on this day.

You never will regret it
'Cause when the day is through
Whatever you have passed along
Returns tenfold to you.

by Evelyn Mika

Youth & Adult Readings and Reflections

ABCs for a Great Thanksgiving

Thanking the Lord is the real beginning of Thanksgiving!
Acknowledge Him: Father, Son, and Holy Spirit
Believe Him
Confess to Him
Desire Him
Eagerly experience His empowering blessing
Find faith in Him
Give Him glory
Hope in Him
Inspired by Him
Joyful in Him
Keep focused on Him
Look to Him, Love Him, Live for Him
Memorize His Word
Need Him
Obey Him
Praise Him, Pray to Him, Point others to Him
Quiet before Him
Receive Him, Rest in Him, Revived in Him
Seek Him as my Savior
Think about Him
Utterly trust Him
Value His Word
Worship Him, now and forever
X – examine His claims
Yearn for His Kingdom
Zealous for Him

by Elaine Hardt

Thank You, Lord, for Loving Me

Inspired by 1 Thessalonians 5:16-18

Thank You, Lord,
For loving me
In the good times
And in the bad;
And in the Spring
And in the Fall
In the Summer
And in the Winter;
And anytime
I don't feel loved,
Even by You!
Thank You, Lord,
For loving me.

Thank You, Lord,
For loving me
When doors shut
In my face;
You hurt with me
All the way.
Thank You, Lord,
For loving me.

Thank You, Lord,
For loving me
For sending Your Son,
Whom You deeply loved,
To suffer and die
For all mankind.
Despite my unworthiness
Thank You, Lord,
For loving me
That much!

by Gordon Williams

Thankful for God's Love

Have I told You lately that I love You?
And I've neglected to proclaim Your praise!
Your love demonstrated in Jesus,
Father, You have blessed me all my days.

One God, all powerful, eternal,
Beyond anything my mind can conceive;
Redeemer of everyone who calls to You;
I'm grateful You invite me to believe.

I must own up to the truth of my shortcomings;
My own efforts cannot this sin erase,
But You have made forgiveness possible.
I would be lost without Your grace.

Have I told You lately that I love You?
Heavenly Father, I'm telling You now.

You are Creator of the universe,
You've made it all, I don't understand how;
You've been my Provider and Protector,
Oh yes, I love You; I'm telling You now.

Before me lies life's mystery of death,
So soon I will pass from here to there;
How I long to see You in true reality,
And face to face, my love declare.

by Elaine Hardt

What Happened to Thanksgiving

September didn't used to be the start
Of holiday shopping and decoration;
Halloween didn't get this much attention.
Christmas was more about little surprises of love,
Less of expensive expectation.

What in the world happened to Thanksgiving?
Where is the gratitude earnestly expressed,
Appreciating hard work and persistence,
Celebrating God's bountiful hand of blessing?
We have forgotten thankfulness.

In our hurried life we speed through November,
Some will dash right on to December;
Presents to buy, cards to send, parties, and, and, and—
But I for one, will find a quiet place,
Thank God for His mercy and wondrous grace.

by Elaine Hardt

My Prayer of Thankfulness

Dear Heavenly Father,
The world outside my door is calling
But my heart longs for a quiet talk with You.
Your Word says to pray and seek Your presence, so I do.
Thank You for letting me know about You.
How awesome You are!
Such power, such wisdom is displayed in the universe.
Your creations dazzle my imagination.
Open my eyes to see these wonders.
How merciful You are!
To bring us to eternal life You paid an incredible price.
Jesus leads us to repentance and forgiveness.
Save me from my sins and foolish ways.
How good You are!
Your grace enables me to become Your child by faith
And empowers me to live day by day for You.
Make something beautiful and useful out of my life.
How loving You are!
There is life eternal in heaven after this brief life is over,
And You give me the strong desire to trust in You.
Shine Your love through me to others.
How holy and just You are!
An end to the devastation and misery of sin is at hand.
All evil will be banished at Your coming.
Nothing contrary to Your will can stand.
I take comfort in knowing You and Your intentions.
I lay down my worries and fears, my doubts and confusion.
I receive from Your hand all that I need for today,
Wisdom, strength, confidence, and joy.
Touch my physical body with healing.
Give me victory over testings and temptations.
For all Your blessings I will sing and give thanks.
It is my privilege to work today in Your presence.
Thank You for being my wonderful Heavenly Father.
Amen.

by Elaine Hardt

Our Heritage

For those who came before us,
Our Founding Fathers brave,
We give our thanks and gratitude
For the guidance they always gave.
We remember the principles
They held to be so true,
And try to keep their values alive
In everything we do.

by Dorothy Heibel

Recipe for Thanksgiving

Editor's Note: Give this personal reflection out to each person present at church on the Sunday nearest Thanksgiving.

This free, no-calorie recipe can't be beat for simplicity and good results. It's just what every busy person needs, and this means you! Go ahead, indulge yourself.

1. Close your eyes and count to 10.
2. As you open your eyes, be thankful you can see. Be thankful you remember your numbers. Be thankful you can speak aloud.
3. Look around. Be thankful for a roof and four walls and a door. Got a bathroom? Be thankful. Food in the fridge? Be thankful.
4. Now, before you get carried away with feeling really good, stop and ask yourself, "Who gave me all these blessings?"
5. Talk to God, out loud if possible. Acknowledge Him as the Creator of everything and Maker of you, in particular. If you haven't been on speaking terms with Him lately, now is the time to remedy that unintended neglect.
6. This is not the time to present Him with a list of what you want for Christmas. This is not the time to whine and complain, either.
7. The purpose of Thanksgiving is to sharpen your skills of awareness of what it means to be alive, and who better to thank than the One you are going to meet when you die.
8. As the day goes on, see how many other things you can be thankful for.
9. By the end of the day look out the window and see the sunset, then look for the stars and moon. Be thankful you live on the only beautiful, inhabitable planet there is.
10. End the day by thanking God for anything else you can think of before falling asleep with a big smile on your face.

Look in the Bible at the many examples of thanking God. Especially in the book of Psalms, read of people calling out to God, talking about His blessings, and giving thanks.

"The LORD is righteous in all his ways and loving toward all he has made. The LORD is near to all who call on him . . ." Psalm 145:17-18

The blessing of Thanksgiving is peace, contentment, appreciation, and deep inner joy. This blessing is a free gift from God, and it comes when we are in a loving relationship with Him. Jesus makes this possible. Read the Gospels in the New Testament to appreciate Him.

You may enjoy this Recipe for Thanksgiving so much you decide to do it every day, or at least one day a week. Call it Sabbath, a rest for the body and soul. When you are thankful you are bringing a blessing upon yourself, as well as giving God respect and honor that is due Him.

by Elaine Hardt

Scripture Readings

by Beth Westcott

Choral reading of Scripture is an alternative to the often toneless reading of Scripture during a worship service. The blend of voices, using changes of inflection, volume, and pitch, allows us to gain a new appreciation for Scripture reading and to discover new things in Scripture. Alternating men's and women's voices, light and dark voices, solos, duets, etc., is fun, challenging, and it allows more people to be involved.

As in singing, practice is important for the Scripture Choir. One or two practices may be enough to allow the speakers to become familiar with the Scripture passages and to learn to read together.

Using the Psalms and other praise and thanksgiving passages from Scripture is a good way to celebrate Thanksgiving as part of a worship service. A Scripture Choir is suitable for any size church.

Thanksgiving Scripture Choir

Psalm 145 KJV

MEN: I will extol thee, my God, O king;

WOMEN: and I will bless thy name

ALL: for ever and ever.

MEN: Every day will I bless thee;

WOMEN: And I will praise thy name

ALL: for ever and ever.
Great is the LORD, and greatly to be praised; and his greatness is unsearchable.

MEN'S DUET: One generation shall praise thy works to another,

WOMEN'S DUET: and shall declare thy mighty acts.

SOLO 1: I will speak of the glorious honor of thy majesty,

SOLO 2: and of thy wondrous works.

SOLO 3: And men shall speak of the might of thy terrible acts:

SOLO 4: and I will declare thy greatness.

MEN'S DUET: They shall abundantly utter the memory of thy great goodness,

WOMEN'S DUET: and shall sing of thy righteousness.

SOLO 1: The LORD is gracious, and full of compassion;

SOLO 2: slow to anger, and of great mercy.

SOLO 3: The LORD is good to all:

SOLO 4: and his tender mercies are over all his works.

MEN: All thy works shall praise thee, O LORD;

WOMEN: and thy saints shall bless thee.

MEN: They shall speak of the glory of thy kingdom,

WOMEN: and talk of thy power;

WOMEN'S DUET: To make known to the sons of men his mighty acts,

MEN'S DUET: and the glorious majesty of his kingdom.

BOTH DUETS: Thy kingdom is an everlasting kingdom,

ALL: and thy dominion endureth throughout all generations.

SOLO 1: The LORD upholdeth all that fall,

SOLO 2: and raiseth up all those that be bowed down.

SOLO 3: The eyes of all wait upon thee;

SOLO 4: and thou givest them their meat in due season.

WOMEN'S DUET: Thou openest thine hand,

MEN'S DUET: and satisfiest the desire of every living thing.

ALL: The LORD is righteous in all his ways,

WOMEN: and holy in all his works.

ALL: The LORD is nigh unto all them that call upon him,

MEN: to all that call upon him in truth.

SOLO 1: He will fulfill the desire of them that fear him:

SOLO 2: he also will hear their cry, and will save them.

SOLO 3: The LORD preserveth all them that love him:

SOLO 4: but all the wicked will he destroy.

MEN: My mouth shall speak the praise of the LORD;

WOMEN: and let all flesh bless his holy name

ALL: for ever and ever.

Choral Reading for Thanksgiving—Scripture Choir

Psalm 67:3-7 KJV

WOMEN: Let the people praise thee, O God;
let all the people praise thee.

MEN: O let the nations be glad and sing for joy:
for thou shalt judge the people righteously,
and govern the nations upon earth.

WOMEN: Let the people praise thee, O God;

MEN: let all the people praise thee.

WOMEN: Then shall the earth yield her increase;

MEN: and God, even our own God, shall bless us.

WOMEN: God shall bless us;

MEN: and all the ends of the earth shall fear him.

Psalm 92:1-2, 4 KJV

DUET 1: It is a good thing to give thanks unto the LORD,

DUET 2: and to sing praises to thy name, O most High:

DUET 1: To shew forth thy lovingkindness in the morning,

DUET 2: and thy faithfulness every night.

SOLO 1: For thou, LORD, hast made me glad through thy work:

SOLO 2: I will triumph in the works of thy hands.

Psalm 103:1-5 KJV

SOLO 1: Bess the LORD, O my soul:

SOLO 2: and all that is within me,

SOLOS 1 & 2: bless his holy name!

SOLO 1: Bless the LORD, O my soul,

SOLO 2: and forget not all his benefits:

SOLO 3: Who forgiveth all thine iniquities;

SOLO 4: who healeth all thy diseases;

SOLO 5: Who redeemeth thy life from destruction;

SOLO 6: who crowneth thee with lovingkindness and tender mercies;

SOLO 7: Who satisfieth thy mouth with good things;

SOLO 8: so that thy youth is renewed like the eagle's.

Psalm 104:33-35 KJV

SOLO 1: I will sing unto the LORD as long as I live:
I will sing praise to my God while I have my being.

SOLO 2: My meditation of him shall be sweet:
I will be glad in the LORD.

SOLOS 1 & 2: . . . Bless thou the LORD, O my soul

ALL: Praise ye the LORD.

Ephesians 5:18b-20 KJV

ALL: " . . . be filled with the Spirit;

SOLO 1: Speaking to yourselves in psalms and hymns and spiritual songs,

SOLO 2: singing and making melody in your heart to the Lord;

SOLO 3: Giving thanks always for all things unto God and the Father

SOLO 4: in the name of our Lord Jesus Christ."

Programs & Services

A Service of Praise and Thanksgiving

by Dorothy Heibel

Cast:

LEADER
READER 1
READER 2
READER 3
CONGREGATION

Editor's Note: All of the following scripture passages are paraphrased from the *New International Version* of the Bible.

LEADER: "Let us praise the Lord together and exalt His name." (Ps. 34:3)

Song: *We Gather Together*

READER 1: Let your lives overflow with joy and thanksgiving for all He has done. (Col. 2:7)

READER 2: Don't be weary in prayer. Watch for God's answers and be thankful when they come. (Col. 4:2)

READER 3: Don't worry about anything. Instead pray about everything. Tell God your needs and don't forget to thank Him for His answers. (Phil. 4:6)

LEADER: Thank God for His Son—His gift too wonderful for words! (2 Cor. 9:15)

READER 1: What God wants from us is our true thanks. He wants our promises fulfilled. He wants us to trust Him in our times of trouble so He can rescue us and we can give Him glory. (Ps. 50:14-15)

READER 2: Come before Him with thankful hearts. Let us sing Him psalms of praise for the Lord is a Great God, the great King of all gods. Come, kneel before the Lord, our Maker for He is our God. (Ps. 95:2, 6-7)

READER 3: Go through His open gates with thanksgiving; enter His courts with praise. Give thanks to Him and bless His name. (Ps. 100:4)

LEADER: Oh, give thanks to the Lord, for He is good. His lovingkindness continues forever. (Ps. 136)

Responsive Reading: Psalm 136

READER 1: Give thanks to the Lord of lords.

CONGREGATION: For His lovingkindness continues forever.

READER 2: Praise Him who alone does mighty miracles.

CONGREGATION: For His lovingkindness continues forever.

READER 3: Praise Him who made the heavens.

CONGREGATION: For His lovingkindness continues forever.

READER 1: Praise Him who planted the water within the earth.

CONGREGATION: For His lovingkindness continues forever.

READER 2: Praise Him who made the heavenly lights.

CONGREGATION: For His lovingkindness continues forever.

READER 3: The sun to rule the day and the moon and stars at night.

CONGREGATION: For His lovingkindness continues forever.

READER 1: He gives food to every living thing.

CONGREGATION: For His lovingkindness continues forever.

READER 2: Give thanks to the God of heaven.

EVERYONE: For His lovingkindness continues forever.

CONGREGATION: Amen! Blessing and glory and wisdom and thanksgiving and honor and power and might be to our God forever and ever. Amen. (Rev. 7:12)

Hymn: *Now Thank We All Our God* or *For the Beauty of the Earth*

(The following poem may be used during the service or as a separate offering.)

A Thanksgiving Prayer to the Savior

When things go wrong, Lord,
Give us a song
To sustain us
And carry us through.

When sorrows surround
And troubles abound,
Let's remember to turn
To You.

A simple prayer
Will lift our soul
And turn the wrong
To right.

Though dark be the way
And weary the day,
Christ will carry us
Into the light.

Give Thanks to the Lord

by Beth Westcott

Prelude

Scripture Choir: Psalm 19:1 NIV

SOLO READER: "The heavens declare the glory of God;
The skies proclaim the work of his hands."

Welcome

Announcements

Opening Prayer

Solo: *Thank You, Lord* (Ron Hamilton, Majesty Music, Inc.)

Scripture Choir: Psalm 47:1-2, 6-7 NIV

ALL: "Clap your hands, all you nations;
shout to God with cries of joy.

MEN: How awesome is the LORD Most High,
The great King over all the earth!

WOMEN: Sing praises to God, sing praises;
sing praises to our King, sing praises.

ALL: For God is the King of all the earth;
sing to Him a psalm of praise."

Children's Choir: *Clap Your Hands* (Jimmy Owens/Carol Owens, Bud John Songs, Inc.)

Scripture Choir: 1 Chronicles 16:8-12 NIV

SOLO 1: "Give thanks to the LORD,

SOLO 2: call on His name;

SOLO 3: make known among the nations

SOLOS 1, 2, 3: what he has done.

WOMEN: Sing to him,

MEN: sing praise to him;

ALL: tell of all his wonderful acts.

MEN: Glory in his holy name;

WOMEN: let the hearts of those who seek the LORD

ALL: rejoice.

MEN: Look to the LORD and his strength;

WOMEN: seek his face always.

SOLO 1: Remember the wonders he has done,

SOLO 2: his miracles,

SOLO 3: and the judgments he pronounced."

Hymn: *Sing Praise to God*

Offering

Praise and Prayer

Scripture Choir: 1 Chronicles 16:23-34 NIV

ALL: "Sing to the LORD, all the earth;
proclaim his salvation day after day.

MEN: Declare his glory among the nations,

WOMEN: his marvelous deeds among all peoples.

MEN: For great is the LORD

WOMEN: and most worthy of praise;

SOLO 1: he is to be feared above all gods.

SOLO 2: For all the gods of the nations are idols,

SOLOS 1, 2: but the LORD made the heavens.

SOLO 3: Splendor and majesty are before him;

SOLO 4: strength and joy in his dwelling place.

SOLOS 3, 4: Ascribe to the LORD,

SOLOS 1-4: O families of nations,

DUET 1: ascribe to the LORD glory and strength,

DUET 2: ascribe to the LORD the glory due his name.

MEN: Bring an offering

WOMEN: and come before him;

ALL: worship the LORD
in the splendor of his holiness.

MEN: Tremble before him, all the earth!

WOMEN: The world is firmly established;

ALL: it cannot be moved.

SOLO 1: Let the heavens rejoice,

SOLO 2: let the earth be glad;

SOLO 3: let them say among the nations,

SOLO 4: 'The LORD reigns!'

DUET 1: Let the sea resound, and all that is in it;

DUET 2: let the fields be jubilant,

DUET 1, 2: and everything in them!

WOMEN: Then the trees of the forest will sing,
they will sing for joy before the LORD,

MEN: For he comes to judge the earth.

WOMEN: Give thanks to the LORD,

MEN: for he is good;

ALL: His love endures forever."

Choir: *The Trees of the Field* (Rubin/Dauermann, Lillenas Publishing Co.)

Scripture Choir/Congregation: Psalm 95:1-7 NIV *para*

ALL: Oh, come, let us sing to the Lord!
Let us shout joyfully to the Rock of our salvation.

WOMEN: Come, let us sing for joy to the Lord;

MEN: Let us shout aloud to the Rock of our salvation

MEN: and extol Him with music and song.

WOMEN: For the Lord is the great God,

MEN: the great King above all gods.

WOMEN: In His hand are the depths of the earth,

MEN: and the mountain peaks belong to Him.

WOMEN: The sea is His, for He made it;

MEN: And His hands formed the dry land.

WOMEN: Come, let us bow down in worship,

MEN: let us kneel before the Lord our Maker.

ALL: For He is our God,
and we are the people of His pasture,
the flock under His care.

Choir: *Worship the Lord* (Ron Hamilton, Majesty Music, Inc.)

Just What *Is* Praise?

by Vicki S. Meier

Cast:

LEADERS
PERSON 1—Member of congregation
PERSON 2—Member of congregation
PERSON 3—Member of congregation
PERSON 4—Member of congregation

LEADER *(on platform preparing to lead service):* This evening we are coming together to praise the Lord. What a privilege it is to be able to praise Him! And what better day to do that than on the Sunday before Thanksgiving, giving praise for His many blessings and goodness to us.

PERSON 1 *(standing):* Excuse me! Excuse me! I'm here, and I'm always hearing the phrase "praising the Lord" in church. Just what *is* praise anyway?

PERSON 2 *(standing):* I know what it is! It's when we sing, you know, those really spiritual songs. Not those fast, lighthearted ones. You know the ones I mean—the heavy, more serious and deeply moving music. *(Sings slowly and solemnly)* "Praise God from Whom all blessings flow . . . *(drags out the word "flooww")* Praise Him all creatures here . . ."

PERSON 3 *(interrupts from congregation):* No, no, no, that's not praise. To be truly praising you have to have both your hands in the air *(demonstrates while singing)*. See? Like this . . . Lifting your hands towards heaven . . . *(sings with hand raised high and swaying back and forth while singing)* "Hosanna, hosanna. Hosanna in the highest."

PERSON 4 *(speaking up):* You both have it all wrong. Praising God happens when we get down on our knees and pray a sincere heartfelt prayer. And to be truly effective, the lower and deeper your voice, the better you praise. Let me demonstrate— *(slow, bass voice)* "Our Father in heaven, we praise You today for Your love, and we praise You for Your goodness . . ."

LEADER: Hold on now. Wait just a minute. I think you have some misconceptions of what praising God is all about. Praise is more than a song we sing, or the words we say. It's a lifestyle—a life that reflects God in our everyday walk, and attitude, and our talk.

(LEADER *proceeds to give following points regarding praise using the individual letters of the word "praise." It is very effective if using a slide presentation to present the following points. Can either read as is, or elaborate on each section.)*

Praise Is:

Preparation (Rev. 3:20)—Opening our hearts to hear the still small voice of God speaking to us; preparing our minds to be receptive to what the Holy Spirit has for us each and every day; being receptive to His presence and guidance.

Prayer (Matt. 6:6)—Not pretentious prayers, but time spent alone with God in the quiet place; a time of communion with Him—listening to the voice of God and allowing Him to speak to us. Being in an attitude of prayer 24 hours a day whether it be in the car, at work, shopping, in a restaurant, wherever we may be. God is as close as the whisper of His name.

Praise Is:

Rejoicing (Phil. 4:4)—Being grateful for God's many blessings; looking for God's goodness in our lives, and recognizing His faithfulness no matter what, or in spite of, our circumstances.

Reaching (Isa. 52:7)—Sharing God's love and the good news of the gospel with the world around us; extending the same hand of love, mercy, and forgiveness that God has extended to us.

Praise Is:

Acknowledging (Ps. 95:6; James 4:7)—Humbly accepting the sovereignty of God, His majesty, and His power; surrendering totally in faith to an unseen, but completely trustworthy, Lord; giving our all to Him and resting on His promises.

Allowing (Matt. 7:21)—Saying "Yes!" to God's will in our lives; allowing Him to use us as He sees fit in the work of His Kingdom: letting go of our own understanding and giving ourselves as an offering to Him, believing that God equips each and every one of us for the task He wants us to fulfill.

Praise Is:

Inviting (Prov. 11:30)—Bringing that loved one, or friend, or co-worker to church worship; coming alongside that one who needs a Christian friend, or confidante, or mentor; assimilating others into the fellowship of Christ and His church; living such a life of holiness that your very lifestyle and behavior invites others to know Jesus as the personal Savior.

Ignoring (Phil. 3:12-14)—The world and its pull on our hearts; turning aside from anything that would draw us away from God; intentionally choosing to follow Christ, even in the face of persecution; keeping our eyes on Him, neither turning to the left or the right.

Praise Is:

Sacrificing (Matt. 6:33; Luke 14:27)—Giving up our wants and wishes to those of our Heavenly Father; being willing to eliminate those activities in our lives that would prevent God from being first; rearranging the priorities in our lives—taking time for prayer and meditation, evangelistic endeavors, and church worship; releasing control of our time, talent, service, and giving to Him.

Seeking (1 Chron. 28:9; Isa. 55:6)—God's Word states that we shall find Him when we seek Him with all our hearts; developing a close, intimate, personal relationship with God; longing for the utmost our Lord has to offer; having an unquenchable hunger and thirst for the things of God.

Praise Is:

Exhibiting (Phil. 1:27)—Let the beauty of Jesus be seen in us; exhibiting the attributes of Christ; the fruits of the Spirit being revealed in our personal, everyday living; lives that point to Jesus through our love, kindness, compassion, gentleness, forbearance, and so forth.

Enjoying (1 Tim. 6:17)—Enjoying the journey called life; God's joy being viewed in us; may others see a peace and a contentment that goes beyond all normal human understanding; seeing a strength and courage beyond our own ability; being illuminated from within with inexpressible happiness.

Genuine praise is all of this and more. Now let's lift our hearts and voices in praise to Him!

(Close service with song of praise and thanksgiving.)